THE VIOLET ROOM

THE VIOLET ROOM

JULIE WHITBY

ACUMEN PUBLICATIONS
1994

Acknowledgements are due to the following magazines in which some of these poems first appeared: *Acumen, Agenda, Contemporary Review, Country Life, The Countryman, Encounter, Littack, Magma, Outposts, The Scotsman, T.L.S., Tribune,* and in *Agenda Anthology* (published by Carcanet); *Big Little Poem Card Series; Homage to Imagism* (Published by AMS Press, New York); and *Turret Books*

Copyright © Julie Whitby 1994

British Library Cataloguing-in-Publication Date:
A catalogue record for this book is available
from the British Library.

ISBN: 1 – 873161 – 06 – 9

Published by:
ACUMEN PUBLICATIONS
6 The Mount
Higher Furzeham
Brixham
South Devon
TQ5 8QY

Printed by :
Herbert Robinson
Ilkeston, Derbyshire, DE 7 8EF

for Dick — and to the memory of my parents.

CONTENTS

The Violet Room   3
In Adversity   5
All The Long Day   6
Off-Stage   7
London's Theme   8
Lincoln's Inn Fields   9
In Kingsway, Holborn   10
Point Of Departure   11
Gift   12
Prayer   13
Obsession: prelude and three movements   14
Remembering Harry   16
Solo Vision   17
Fool's Gold   18
Postscript   19
May Night In Brighton   20
Voices   21
Sketch Of A Psychiatrist   22
Russian Collage   23
Messages   24
Revenant   25
Imagining Daffodils   26
Blossom In The Air   27
Always   28
No More The Old Sadness   29
Leaving Him To Sleep   30
Mulberry Tree   31
"It's Only Meanwhile"   32
Summer's Ending   33
Season Of Mists   34
Exile   35
Temples   36
After "The Road In Louveciennes"   37

THE VIOLET ROOM

The violet room, they called it,
yet we knew otherwise.

Misty, violet curtains hung there:
moistly welcoming, oh yes.

But through their careful lies
we sensed its sumptuous secrets,

judged them dear as wild strawberries,
lay in wait for lurid hints:

an uncut novel in French—
scrumptiously virginal—

and smelling superb to us
as croissants and coffee.

The aroma of tobacco,
not Papa's surely?

A drawer crackling with lace petticoats,
unworn. Why? What for?

Our days had a point, a purpose:
we waited, bided our time.

But nothing decisive
was ever discovered.

We consoled ourselves finally
with Enid Blyton, Jane Austen. Or, unabashed,

tried on Mamma's lipstick
in the dusty mirror of that ghosted room.

At other times wept copiously,
without knowing why, hollow as our dolls.

The violet room we call it now,
yet they know otherwise.

IN ADVERSITY

At peace with the world:
all my leaves unfurled.
Sweet this audacity!
Not yet the catastrophe.

ALL THE LONG DAY

(For my mother)

I wake to the desolation
of knowing I'll not see you again.
How unfeelingly then I treated you,
how fiercely tender I've since become.

All the long day
your love flowed without hesitation—
but my stupid heart lay numb.

Now I wake to a stormy desolation:
through clouds of memory, of remorse,
sense the blue of dawn cannot return,
has tunelessly changed to dun.

OFF-STAGE

Lost in a foreign land
I long to act,
and don't want to act, abhor it,
would rather watch the river swirl.
Is this all because your hand
is no longer there
beside my own?

Lamplight fixes me
with its tallow, off-colour stare.
Clouds swallow me up.

I am not at home
on the well-worn tracks
of this unsyncopated life
I'm pacing—
yet the intoxicating shock of the stars!
I do not belong here.

Even love is quite different
inside myself.
It doesn't wear
hat and gloves,
nor go to church.
That check table-cloth, too: all wrong.

But on the wall there's a print:
trees with their playful gold umbrellas.
I'm in the white-brown bark, I think,
or among flaming leaves on the ground,
crackling at a stranger's touch,
an unknown footstep,
lost in a foreign land.

LONDON'S THEME

Theatrical city of leaves,
of domes, and murky treacheries:
sly, cold river, the unknown serpent you fear,
stars fluttering in brilliance of blue-pink skies
are the eyes of the one you long for,
who inhabits another city
and knows you not. Neither you, nor I—
sapphire-flashing city of dreams that deceive.

LINCOLN'S INN FIELDS:
HOME TO THE HOMELESS

A purple blanket under filigree leaves,
soft April petals pink the grass that's floor—
not quite the idyll that it was before:
a homeless pair about a brazier shift their feet.

It's noisier now that dusk is here.
They're out from tents which strew sheer grass.
Or from wherever, wherever else
bare days are shivered through.

A man checks half-a-dozen blankets,
prepares methodically for night,
as pigeons (pastoral) coo and ghostly, white,
tulips quaintly bless an eerie scene

(on the night that Messiaen and Francis Bacon died).
More wood is piled upon the fire
till its mesmeric banner reaches higher
than a child of ten could leap

as it crackles in its sexual trance.
At a closer look, those tulips are skeletal,
picked by birds. And now a van like an ambulance
arrives. They gather unmistakably: food?

But its clothes they're handling, greedily.
I've had enough, it's getting chilly.
Not quite the idyll that it was before,
I'll head for home. And for the first time—
look—a rat is leading the way.

IN KINGSWAY, HOLBORN

She sat outside the soot-grey church
old dishevelled, brown,
and grubby, of course.
Slate-grey pigeons messed the steps around,
the colour of despondency.

Averting my gaze automatically,
I promised I'd come back to ask
"Are you O.K.?" The converse
seemed obvious, blatant as a hearse,
nor did I return: not on my way.

Yet at night when sleep is hard to find
that dismal cameo itself returns:
church, hag, pigeons—a trio
tuned like sleet on a winter's day
and fixed as a brooch to my mind.

This much is certain, she's no recent refugee
fled from Balkan atrocity
but a home-grown cockney catastrophe,
her only friend the wind.
For sins of omission, easy to commit,
pray for us now and at the hour of our death—
in Holborn or Tahiti.

POINT OF DEPARTURE:
CANALETTO'S BRIDGE OF SIGHS

Will you ever meet me on the bridge of sighs?
I'm swaying there already. At least the view from here
is Canaletto's: exquisite, rare.
Unreal it must be too, though not altogether lies—
and yet you've never as much as glanced into my eyes.
Just looked away with that cold stare:
London. Bleak, grey ... my colours are his. "Beware,"
I should have whipped myself when first I felt those ties
of longing tenderness entangling me.
But tired Cupid seemed so old a friend: harmless,
a boy locked away in antiquity's tomb.
Though now, can't you meet me half-way on this
                          bridge of sighs? Charmless,
you've charmed me. Before wrinkles are frequent
                              as stars in love's sky,
eat of the lotus, lose all desire for home!

GIFT

The tree jangles her laughing green and gold leaves
with the delicacy of a Debussy,

but her trunk has all the necessary toughness
of a seasoned artist.

Yet at this distance, it hasn't that starkness
of the naked, unloved human.

Her bark seems softened, or roughened,
by the constant, affectionate touch of wind and rain.
I would not carve your name there.

Rather I will tell you where she stands,
lightly embraced—enhanced by the blue air—
her leaves in perpetual, fascinating motion,

like my thoughts forever
helplessly centred around you.

Remember this tree, then,
as an expression, a vision

of what I can never be,
can never give,

whose form nonetheless encompasses
all my own chequered feelings:
jangling like her green and gold leaves.

PRAYER

Send me sleep, gentle as pollen in the wind.
Let the tireless galloping of mind cease.
Mind grandly, miraculously turned
Tchaikovsky's first concerto!
Allow my swans tomorrow will be geese.
Let me find the soft pedal soon
before décolleté night, replete with attractive vices—
her garlic and cinnamon spices—
corrupts as she caresses, disintegrates.
Let me quietly unwind her fleece in dreams.
Cool sleep, descend.

OBSESSION:
Prelude and Three Movements .

Like a poppy on fire in a cornfield
I wait for you to pluck me,
hold me to your heart.
Then—oh how gently—tear me
petal by petal, apart.

Your face arouses tenderness,
your voice desire,
but your touch scatters stars.
Lacking your love, I am helpless
as an actress without a play,
as sky without earth to dream over.
When I wake you are here,
and in the dark, also.
Desire for you is a shimmering shawl
I have worn all winter and summer,
yet now it scarcely covers my body ...

why is it I should want
your secret, porcelain face?
Why sweetly important

to feel our bodies touch?
They don't. And I've grown stale
with waiting: talking so much

to you that I wonder,
cold one, do my thoughts reach you,
touch you, slyly wander

close, as I still yearn to do?
Or is this unholy imagination, too —
like my unruly daily desire for you?

Like a white mist in the evening
desire swathes my being,

like music in the mind, unplayed,
your name on my lips,

the hope that one night you'll love me,
like a smile on the face of the moon.

Let it be soon. For the moon's brightness hurts
and time is shaking his leaves.

Like a white mist in the evening
you steal upon my being,

like music in the mind unplayed,
like a smile on the face of the moon.

REMEMBERING HARRY

(For my father)

The piano consoles itself with notes ...
since my loss of you is final, I search
uneasy semiquavers to recall
a trace
       if not your quintessence,
but like desultory leaves
whirling out of sight
just as one reaches them,
your face
       dingily hovers on the doorstep of consciousness,
never daring to disturb
grief lodged by time.

If I gently pushed the door,
would I let your ghost in?
Winter and war nod their heads.
You smile behind glasses,
shake the snow from your feet
as Christmases before,
raise a glass to "absent friends"—
I shiver at your laugh.
Now the wine of violins is the background for all this.
"L'chayim" you murmur, from wherever you are.

SOLO VISION

Those old school gates are ahead of us now
as we linger in the back of a car:
my father, darkly handsome gypsy-fashion,
tells me he's mentioned in Mayakovsky,
"Solo Vision," or something like that.
He's mildly pleased. Would I like some fruit?
My hug is clumsy, affectionate. But then I see

a too-huge moon whose brilliance terrifies—
striking that mortality chord as surely as a clock.
"Oh I never get tired" he smiles, looking shyly wise.
Perhaps he'll make ninety? Or beyond. I'm unaware
this is merely a dream, if beautiful, rare ...
I rejoice at the chance of his company again.

FOOL'S GOLD

If I could choose to meet you
on such a day as this:
grass green as desire,
yellow gold of daffodil,
sky a holy blue,

you would not then refuse
my jewellery of glances—
taut with wishes, kisses
unbestowed. But my companion is
that motherly sun, alone.

You've parcelled up the moon.

POSTSCRIPT

If I were to speak to you
in the ordinary way
there'd be a wall of snow between
what I feel and what I'd (frostily) say:

words, like the trivial froth of waves
that have almost reached the shore and safety,
telling little of the ocean's troubled roar.

Thus postcards brag of the everyday,
not of the way your face and body stay—
when the dross of the day has drifted away—
like secret bluebells in unvisited woods.

MAY NIGHT IN BRIGHTON

Dazed wisps of cloud:
angel floss to a child,
but this is an adult hour; the wind is crass.

Papers totter across the road
idle as bewildered dreams, or praise.
I listen with awe for each heartbeat,

I wait for poems to float from windows—
explicit as an actress undressing—
for it is late.

And now the wind caresses expectantly
and there are parties blossoming into the street.
Soon a multitude of cats beckon plumply

with greenly spell-bound eyes.
(Why does the world close his eyes so early?)
Then scythe the night with their howls

of bitter sex, her pain.
It is late. So much unsaid:
erased by the smiling rain.

VOICES

Oppressed by the small talk of prose:
that spotty, short back and sides too garrulous clerk,
I long for the terse, yet provocative Muse.
Sister, perfumed and poised, rippling
with musical nuance, I've missed you so harshly
the day's grown dark:
your eyes loquacious with feeling,
in your hair the ghost of a rose.

While prose plods and stumbles,
takes one hundred pages or so
to unbutton his flies,
she tells without explaining.
Flies over continents with a choice remark
and pertinent: her form supple with rhythm and meanings,
her perfume rhyme—the truth of colourful lies.

SKETCH OF A PSYCHIATRIST

After long years, I see you sitting there.
Perhaps a fraction older, more obese.
Discourteous and seldom kind, your hair
already gone; in place a smile, a crease.
But humour of a sort there was, if crude,
you'd laugh at length at your own wit, "Poor girl,
she's got the clap again." Little less lewd
seemed to amuse. Despite all this, a whirl
of nerves, of pleasant expectation, I
await your pompous entrance: dry, morose,
your face a careful mask which melancholy
pierces, though nothing else. Yet now, how close
we've drawn, our half-forgotten battles done:
affection and sadness, these two have won.

RUSSIAN COLLAGE

That year I took Autumn as a friend:
nostalgia was in my house.
Yet when I reached you from Vladivostok
on the telephone,
I was ecstatic! I knock at you, I knock,
I try to wake you—
and this was only a wound
with a little cloud of torture over it.

Meanwhile and slowly, I submit
to the blackmail of circumstance:
nostalgia was in my house.
In broadbrimmed hats and long overcoats,
with whole notebooks full of your poems,
long, long ago you crumbled to ashes,
like leafless lilac branches.
That year I took Autumn as my friend.

MESSAGES

There are so many wild flowers in the garden:
yellow-green sighs, brown velvet perfumes,
and mostly they remain—they must—
untouched, unpicked, unknown.

So many shelves in our houses
stacked with unspoken thoughts,
but who will want or dare to read them?

The lights of the plane are winking their message,
blinking back tears, perhaps,
and no-one is listening.

While the harp in the woods is far from silent,
but we are sleeping still
as we mouth our verbiage.

Only in dreams do we embrace the stranger
who is intimately known to us,
and when we awake, cold and shivering,
the silence has been broken by one brief phrase of a song:
yellow-green sighs, brown velvet perfume.

REVENANT

Who is it rustling in the other room
while I lie half-asleep and trying to wake?
It's my mother, came back for things she forgot to take
when she left us. Can death be final as it seems?
Or is it the other way round? Her hair's still wispy,
and such a beautiful blue-gold dress she's wearing,
I wish she'd had one like that. But her pain
is tearing the blankets from off me.
"Remember France?" I'd whispered,
at last. "Oh it's so long ago," she shivered.
I try to pretend it felt "like yesterday"—
unconsoled she'd gone, with the past.
The slates are blue and silver with rain
and look at those drops on the bright-black gutter.
It's too late now to catch the train for London.

IMAGINING DAFFODILS

I shall imagine there are fresh flowers
in my vase which has the dead, blood-red anemones
hanging down; that you are here with me
to feel the sun light up our room with promises.
Look, those floating mountains, the elation
of white untroubled cloud, in a sky
that seems to enter through our windows—
tall, flower-petalled, as in a chapel
meet for love. You've been awake for hours,
my hand on your tum, all dreams have been told,
and now, who's getting some ritual tea?
The green is starting to show on our trees,
shall we sit in the garden, hand in hand,
and kiss now and then as we have done for years?

You, confined to bed in a poky room:
alone. Are you getting enough to eat?
Yes, it's begun to rain. But I shan't succumb
to loneliness, while half-watching on T.V.
all we already knew about
the dismal unemployed, or heart disease,
even though it's highly possible
the poetic progeny's more impressive.
No: I'll keep the day as rounded
as when, your head upon my breast,
we opened the morning together. Shall I read you
this poem? What better beginning. Believing you're here
has got to be easier than playing Electra. After all,
I must have learnt something at that
                              punitive Drama School.

BLOSSOM IN THE AIR

Blossom in the air:
the whole light day a prayer,
when those we love lie ill,
and fear cannot rest still.

Sweetness we have known
may itself atone—
undo—one long night of fear,
when those we love are gone?

ALWAYS

Listening to the rain together—
unravelling the sea:
we who have lain together
for a brief eternity.

NO MORE THE OLD SADNESS

Together we welcome the day—
no more the old sadness—
two ships calm in the bay
yet bright with their journeying.

Together we embrace our day:
bodies close and loving,
green light of trees mingles with sun,

we drink our honied tea at ease, in freedom,
for time has only just begun.
Who could ask for more?
Two ghosts flit across the floor.

LEAVING HIM TO SLEEP

Leaving him to sleep
I journey on
past red-brown ferns and pines
to an unknown destination:
reaps a gentle harvest
the touch of his body warm on mine,
holds its imprint softly there,
as trees and flowers hurtle by
and are soon in mists, behind.
But I shall keep
his sleeping image awake and dear
until I reach
that shuttered destination where
the silent woods are thoughtful,
and we are robbed of thought.

MULBERRY TREE

You placed a mulberry in my mouth
"For True Love's sake," or some such
quip. It hadn't ripened, tasted sharp:
not promising too much.

Yet now when I pass a mulberry tree
I glimpse us as we used to be,
and muse on all the years between—
how strange love's slow sweet ripening.

"IT'S ONLY MEANWHILE,"
the poetry lecturer said
of his immaculate stage-set room

We all live *meanwhile:*

eternally hoping for
cards, events, flowers
that never or seldom happen,

as we pray for a
present or future
that is succulent, superb.

Only the lives of others
appear
without agony, flawless.

Yet nothing—in love—can equal
that grammar of the past,
intangible:

when trees and sky
combined to sigh
the perfect tense away, gone by.

SUMMER'S ENDING

Scent of honeysuckle wanes,
is there no-one in the garden?
You are near but body's haunted:
memories' untouched feast remains.

Only a cardboard feast remains
and there's no-one in the garden.
You are dear, but love is daunted:
scent of honeysuckle wanes.

SEASON OF MISTS

They are sitting on our bench, the lovers:
quiet and close, as we once used to be—
that incline of the head tells all—

leaves are gold and green with mist between,
as before. Enough. I've not the heart to watch
their easy, sweet-slow harmony: ours.

EXILE

In the garden I am always looking—
unwillingly, in vain—for our ghosts.

All those silk-skinned summers,
autumns sharply sweet
as childhood apples,

where are they? Where are we?

The grass is silent.
Parched leaves wander: half-mad, brown.

Our love is present now
only in nostalgic waltzes, dreamed
in (ink-blue?) purple twilight, or

in the arms, the grace of ballet-girls:

glimpsed through those small windows,
paltry sum of all that remains to us,
each locked-up in a coffin-tight loneliness.

Yet, in that familiar-strange garden,
I am still always looking,

as one blinded only yesterday.

TEMPLES

At Temple station flowers you always gave me:
down-petalled roses, perfumed freesias.
How many years? How many posies? Poses?

And now I pray their ashes may somehow save me
from the river's dark disdain:
from all those manicured ladies, triple-faced lawyers

who look in scorn the other way ...
Love, was it today, or yesterday?
For there's still only you—and the untiring rain.

AFTER "THE ROAD IN LOUVECIENNES"
by Camille Pissarro

Do you remember that road in Louveciennes?
The trees taut with their secrets,
and the road tight with snow?

We were close but not touching, as though
what we had was enough, we already knew
all that we needed to know.

How far from reality the road in Louveciennes!
You, a cypress in your dark green dress,
and I, in what my grandfather might have worn,
quaintly mysterious.

How sure the future seemed on our road in Louveciennes:
a sweet cold apple for us to eat.
Those trees, too, would tell us their secrets,

the snow bless us with blossom—
we were close but not touching,
ignorant of love's need, of the drab tread of years.

Do you remember, oh my love, the road in Louveciennes?
Before it grows dark we must find it somehow,
and clasp each other close, since
only we can weep real unpainted tears.